Don't Be *Afraid* To *Tell*

Don't Be *Afraid* To *Tell*

Valerie Mchale

To order additional copies of this book, contact:
Xlibris LLC
0-800-056-3182
www.xlibrispublishing.co.uk
Orders@xlibrispublishing.co.uk
306414

Contents

Why Am I Writing This Book?

The truth is I suffered a long time, and I did not know what to do. I had all this fear inside, and after I failed five suicide attempts, I had gotten to the point where I didn't care anymore if anyone was going to believe me or not. All I knew was I had to try, so I went to school and told a teacher—and it was the most terrifying thing I have ever done. So I am writing this book to show that what you are going through is not living, it is existing.

I know you don't deserve what you are going through. And I know you can do what needs to be done. But this is not about what I know—it's about what you believe and I hope I can help you to believe in yourself. I will not lie to you—it is not going to be easy to talk about what is happening to you. You might feel ashamed, humiliated, and scared, but I'm sorry to say that it has to be you who tells your story. I know you can do this. I know you are strong enough to do this. You need to do it before it's too late.

Existing has to end before living can begin.

Dedication

I would like to dedicate this book to Conner, who I know will stay on the right path and also to my husband, Hassan, who has stood by me and supported me through the difficult memories.

Things I Have Noticed

Abusers are cowards and pick on the people who are smaller and weaker than themselves; this gives the abuser the ability to overpower, intimidate, and control.

Abusers are normally someone you know and maybe even loved like a family member.

Being abused by a stranger does happen but much less than you think.

Abusers will try to isolate you from your friends; this is one of the ways to try and break you.

Too many abusers kill their victims.

Children will lie to cover up what is really going on not because they want to protect their abuser but because they are scared and confused.

People who have been abused by the same person over a long period of time can start to believe that they are 'in love' with the abuser.

Too many people who have grown up and been abused through their life but have believed that they have had a normal life in turn will then abuse their children.

So many children who have grown up in an abusive household and had not received the help they need are likely to suffer from mental illnesses and/or anger issues.

It brings a tear to my eye to say this one, but unfortunately, it is true. Boys who have been sexually abused by men are much less likely to tell anyone about it because of the embarrassment and the stigma they fear they will attract.

All the things I have said to you are true; I have witnessed them myself and also experienced some of them.

Hear Me

Children, I want you all to be smart,
I'm telling you the truth, and it's from my heart,
Abuse isn't good, it isn't right, it's wrong,
You must put a stop to it or the abuser has won.

You have to be strong,
You have to be smart,
Stop the abuse before it can start,
To mess up your life and tear you apart.

I know it's hard,
I've been there myself,
But if I can do it
So can anyone else.

Being Bullied

If someone is bullying you and calling you names,
Making you feel that you're weak and it pains,
If it makes you feel like you want to cry,
And you're at the point where you want to die,
A secret like this can tear your insides,
Because no one can see the pain it just hides,
You need to tell a neighbour, your mom,
Even a teacher—just tell someone.

I promise you this when you say what's been done,
Things will get better for you very soon,
For once it's out, the bullying will stop,
You will feel much better, and better because,
In time you will be as strong as a rock,
You do deserve it because bad you are *not*.

Being Touched

If someone is trying to touch you
On places you know they're not supposed to,
Shout and scream and don't let them do it,
Instinct is powerful, but you have to use it,
You might feel silly, you might feel scared,
But your secret is one that needs to be shared.

So take a deep breath and hold your head up high,
If you need to cry, it's okay—don't be shy,
You're doing the right thing, I know it's hard,
But now you can start to heal your heart.

Being Beaten

If someone is hurting by punching and kicking,
And you feel like your world is black and it's sinking,
If you think that everything will be all right,
Because the bruises and pain are soon out of sight,
I'm sorry to tell you that abuse isn't right,
So don't put up with it—they're wrong and I'm right,
I know you're scared and terrified, it's true,
But telling someone is down to you,
If it's your farther or even your mother,
Maybe your sister or it could be your brother,
It doesn't matter—just tell on the person who decided to hurt you.

Dilemma

I'm all in bits it's terrible,
I don't know what to do,
The abuse has left me torn and raw,
And I'm hurting through and through.

I know my daddy hitting me,
Is wrong and I hope I will die,
Because dying is so easy,
Than living with Daddy's lie.

I know that telling is down to me,
If they don't believe my story,
I would have to go back home to my daddy,
And he will beat me,
And that's not for me.

The Way It Should Be

A child should grow up all happy and clean,
With a full tummy and a smile that beams.

No child should grow up with a kick or a punch,
Or even being hurt after eating their lunch.

A child should grow up with love and laughter,
Surrounded by friends with their futures getting brighter.

No child should grow up all scared and alone,
Feeling too frightened to even go home.

A child is a precious gift worth so much,
Worth much more than anything you can touch.

No child should be spoken to with a frown,
Being called names and even pulled down.

A child needs love and cuddles galore,
They are our future—we should look after them all.

It's Time for Change

Can you listen up, all you children out there?
Now you know why abusers don't care,
But they are wrong, evil, and sad,
They're messed up in the head and that's bad,
But I know something that the abusers don't,
And that is the strength in your heart you hold,
So use your strength and tell what needs told,
Because the abusers getting away with it is getting so old,
So things can change and it starts with you,
Just be strong and you know what to do.

I'm So Alone

I'm so alone, I need a friend,
I can't go home, you see,
'Cause Mummy and Daddy would hit me and leave me,
So I'm living on the streets.

I'm so alone, I need a friend,
I'm feeling scared in the moonlight,
It's raining here in my cardboard box,
And I'm very hungry tonight.

I'm so alone, I need a friend,
What has become of my life?
I'm curling up under a bush,
I'm saying my prayers tonight.

I'm so alone, I need a friend,
I have nowhere to go,
Please God take me away from here,
I just can't take anymore.

I'm so alone, I need a friend,
God must have been busy last night,
Because I'm still here and I'm scared of the thunder,
But maybe tonight's the night.

I'm so alone, I need a friend,
But no one will help me,
So I am going to jump off a bridge,
And I will drown in the sea.

Oh Lord

Oh Lord, won't you save me from my nasty mummy,
She has her friends come over to sit and talk to me,
And when they're gone she has no time for me.

My guardian angel made a visit to me one day,
Asked me if everything's okay.
I said no, oh no, I will never last the day,
Please help me to get away.

Now I thank you, Lord, for saving me,
From her, my drunken mummy.
You showed me the phone book,
From there a number I took.

Oh Lord, I just want to say,
I got a new Mummy today.
I'm happy because you helped me, Lord,
I'm free at last, I can shout to the world.

How to Tell

So now you know what to do, you want to do it,
Because you're doing it for you,
'So how do I do this?' you ask yourself,
Well, I know the answer because I've done it myself,
The way I did this was easiest for me,
I did not think about what might be.

I woke in the morning, left the house, went to school,
It will be okay it's only school,
Once at school, I found a teacher I liked,
It started off with chit chat,
You know, all polite.

I took a deep breath but soon started to cry,
And within a short time I was drying my eyes,
So now what I need you all to see is,
You can be happy with steps one, two, and three.

So once the abuser has left and gone,
The hard work starts—it might take so long,
'Cause the pain is hard to send away,
But I know you're strong and you'll do it one day.

Take these words that I have to say,
Take them and use them, and use them today.

Harsh Words

I hate you, don't you know?
Do my words torment you so?
I hope they do because they are true,
Now your pain is starting to show.

You're a selfish little rat,
You don't even care about that,
If you did, you would go,
And come back no more,
And let me live my life.

Why can't you run away?
Or get run over by a train?
Do something nice,
Get out of my life,
But save me from all blame.

I can't live with you no more,
So get out of my house, just go,
Don't come back,
I really mean that,
And now I'm closing my door.

Secrets

If you be a good boy,
I will buy you a new toy,
If Nanna asks who hit you,
Tell her it was that little boy.

If you be a good little girl,
I'll take you to surf,
Just don't tell anyone,
How much uncle's love hurts.

I know you love your sister,
I love your sister too,
But imagine what I'd do to her,
If you told anyone the truth.

Your brother cannot save you,
Not from me, you bore,
So why tell him things,
He doesn't need to know?

Invisible

Maybe I'm not real,
Maybe I am dead,
Or could I be just a thought,
In someone else's head.

I don't understand this feeling,
I feel so strange inside,
I feel like I'm grieving,
Yet everyone looks alive.

I thought I was invisible,
But now I know not I,
Because it's only my family,
Who hate to see me alive.

The way my family treat me,
It hurts inside so much,
I think I'm gonna tell someone,
'Cause I need some human love.

Were They Abusing Me Too?

A mother abused a girl I knew,
The girl was her daughter—it's sad but true,
The neighbours all say that they knew,
But the girl did wonder, 'Was that true?'

It started to confuse this girl I knew,
What if the neighbours' words were true?
If they knew, were they too,
Abusing the girl by not telling the truth?

Now the girl wanted to run like a horse,
Away from the people who knew of course,
Because to her they were worse than her mum,
They kept her in hell by not telling anyone.

I Wish

I wish I could wake up and not feel numb,
I wish I could feel the rain on my tongue,
I wish I could feel the warmth of the sun,
I wish I knew how to have fun,
I wish I knew how to laugh and not cry,
I wish my heart did not ache so hard,
I wish I could stop all the pain inside,
I wish the bruises were easy to hide,
I wish someone could hear my cries,
I wish when the sky is dark, I could have light,
I wish I could learn how to live my life,
I wish I was free to learn who I am,
I wish I could escape this evil man.

Scared to Go to Bed

I'm scared to go to bed on a night,
It's not what you think I don't need the light,
But when everyone's asleep,
And the house is all dark,
The monster comes out,
And the fear it starts,
He stands in the shadows,
And pulls on my clothes,
He stands at the bottom of the bed,
And grabs my toes,
He rubs his hands all over my bed,
His head's so close I can feel his nose,
The fear he causes is too much to bear,
And when he breathes,
His breath is like stale air,
He takes his time, he's there all night,
He doesn't leave until it's almost light.

Hate

They say a child does not know hate,
That hate is just a word.

When I was a child, I felt hate,
It was taking over my world.

Hate is such a strong feeling,
And some children really know.

It's so easy to hush a child up,
Without letting them say what they know.

So what I'm trying to say to you,
Is as a child you have the right.

To make an adult listen to you,
And tell them what's not right.

I'm a Shadow

I'm a shadow, I'm evil,
I'll hurt your child,
Lock them up,
'Cause I stood outside.

You can't stop me—this is true,
I've had many victims,
And I'm coming for yours too.

They'll think they're being hurt,
They'll cry and struggle,
But when they don't tell anyone,
I'll know they liked it in my bubble.

I can take them anywhere,
Any time that I want,
Because I'm a shadow,
I can do what I want.

My Job

My dad only talks to me when he's angry,
He's always telling me how life is going to be,
But I don't want what life has planned for me,
There's nothing I can do, so what will be will be.

'I've got no beer left, you little boar,'
So get to work to get me some more,
So I go upstairs after he hits me in the head,
I take a deep breath and lie on my bed.

I lay there feeling like meat or a blob,
I know what's coming 'cause it's my job,
His friend comes in with a great grin,
He tells me to talk soft when I'm talking to him.

He scratches his toes and sits beside me,
I feel so dirty, but I can't stop him looking at me,
When he's finished he goes downstairs,
He leaves me crying and feeling scared.

When there've all been in talked and gone,
I'm left lying there crying and alone,
Soon I'm called, so I go downstairs,
The men want more of this talking game.

I start my job but I start it wrong,
So I get punched in the face, and kicked in the groin,
They're all Dad's friends, whom I try to ignore,
I'm tired and crying and to sleep I must go.

They shout things at me whilst having a go,
You're a dirty boar, but we love you know,
I finish the night with a black eye, a broken rib,
I'm swollen and tired when I'm done.

I just can't live this life anymore,
So I'm going to tell my neighbour, the doctor,
He will help me, I'm sure he will,
For he has a family who are never hurt or blue.

A Brother's Love

A little girl lies in a hospital bed,
She looks so bad, like she's almost dead,
She has a bloody nose, broken ribs, a bust lung,
She's got a shattered leg, and she looks so glum.

She can't breathe on her own—has her time come?
She's lived five years, but there was no fun,
Her big brother has come over and he looks at her,
He's got tears in his eyes but that's no wonder,
Look at what has happened to his little sister.

He knows what to do—he has to save her,
Because if he doesn't, how could he live without her?
This twelve-year-old boy is more of a man,
Than the dad who beat this little angel,
He's got more love in his heart,
Than the mother who didn't protect her.

Now he's got the courage,
To tell the hospital workers,
The truth about his parents
And about all the hurting.

Then and Now

I have suffered the way you now suffer
I have felt the pain you now feel
I have pleaded the way you now plead
I have cried the way you now cry
I have seen the darkness you now see
I have feared the future you now fear
I have lived in the hell you now live
I have welcomed the death you now welcome.

Things will change for the better, then you can start to feel like I felt.

I have felt the warmth inside me that you will feel
I have laughed the way you will laugh
I have felt content the way you will feel content
I have felt safe the way you will feel safe
I have gained the confidence that you will gain
I have felt alive the way you will feel alive.

Teacher

A teacher should want his pupils to learn,
To teach them how to go out in the world,
To prepare them for the job that they want,
To help them understand what's right and what's wrong.

Sometimes it happens that a teacher turns bad,
He makes a pupil fall in love with him and it's sad,
Taking advantage of the pupils he knows,
Is not part of his job, for this I am sure.

It's also wrong if he picks on a child,
Making that child feel less than alive,
Even if a teacher lifts his hands,
It is so bad for the child and their plans.

'Cause if you can't trust a teacher, then who can you trust,
It's less than one in a billion teachers is lost,
So I'm telling you this and it's all that I can,
Tell another teacher, now there's a good plan.

Regret

I feel invisible, it tears me apart,
Nobody loves me—it breaks my heart,
There's no conversation, no one looks my way,
I know I'm existing and living's gone away,
I know there are no bruises,
I'm not torn or sore,
But I'm really hurting and the pain is raw,
All I wish is for someone to see me,
Cuddle and talk and spend time with me.

A neighbour moved in and he was new,
I'd never seen him before when going to school,
This man was neighbourly and friendly to me,
Until the day he sat me on his knee,
That was my life until I gave up the fight,
And I took all the tablets I had in my sight,
So now I've gone things have changed,
My family has even learnt my name,
I wish I knew how things could've been.
This is what I wanted my life to have been
I wish I had talked to somebody first,
Instead of ending my life that felt cursed.

A Mother's Apology

I ignored you, I neglected you,
I treated you bad, it wasn't right,
You said you forgave me,
Inside your words kill me,
It puts a lump in my throat,
When I hear those words,
'You are the best mom in the whole world'
You say them like you mean them,
And I'm sure you do,
But I don't deserve them,
Not coming from you,
So what I am trying to put into words,
Is, baby, I love you,
And you, I don't deserve,
I love you, I need you,
But I don't have the right,
Still I'm saying this to you,
You're the light of my life,
I got the help needed,
To put my head right,
And I know you forgive me,
But it still don't feel right.

Worried Teenager

One single teen has so much on his mind,
He worries so much all of the time,
His worries are important to him, you see,
He worries about what's on TV,
If his phone is twelve months old,
Where he's going on his date with a rose?
When he's late back and sneaks in on tiptoes,
Will he get them new downloads?
Will he be late after school for tea?
He had to put out the bin but forgets,
Oh, how this teenager has some regrets,
He spent all his pocket money on sweets and chips,
He should go to PE but then he quits,
These are the worries that a teenager has,
When living with a family that's nice.

Happiness

Coming home from school makes Sam happy,
It never used to be, but he has a loving family,
He walks in the house and closes the door,
He dose his homework then the chores,
It's his first routine and he moans about it,
But deep down inside he really loves it,
There's warmth in the eyes and a very kind smile,
That tells him tea's in a little while,
'Okay,' he says and goes to change,
But really he plays on computer games
He's confident and cheeky but such a good lad,
If he'd stayed where he was, he might have turned bad.

Turned out Well

I went into foster care and the work began,
It was counselling, talking, and learning to trust some how,
It took some time before my fears were gone,
I even learned to smile and have fun,
I learned how to make choices on my own,
I even learned how to bowl,
For the first time in my life, I loved to come home,
I see my parents once a week,
And I'm so happy, they're happy for me,
They've had help and feel better themselves,
My mom got a job stacking shelves,
So now we're all happy and we can laugh,
We even play games in our contact,
It's all worked out for the best in this case,
And there's no way ever I'd change any of these days.

Foster Carer

Dear foster carer, it's just a short letter,
To let you know my feelings 'cause I've told you never,
When I was broke and hurt inside,
You took me in and helped me thrive,
I was a stranger, and you helped me,
And welcomed me in to your family,
It took us sometime to learn to trust,
It was a lot of work for us,
But we did it and we did it for us,
I would also like to say I'm sorry
For the times I broke trust with everybody,
Those days are gone; I've put them in the past,
The future is going to be the best,
To sum it all up, I need you to know,
I'm sorry foster carer, and I love you so.

Your Future

Now you've decided to put the past behind you and move forward,
I am feeling very proud of you, you must be feeling rewarded,
You've got rid of your old life it seems and now you're feeling sorted,
Your plans for the future and college seem to be getting moulded,
One day you'll be the doctor you've so desperately wanted,
So keep away from drink and drugs and don't let your life get haunted,
If you feel it coming on then find someone to talk it,
So look to the future and never look back, and I know you'll be sorted.

Hold Your Head up High

You've been through so much but hold your head up high,
There's nothing to be ashamed of so don't be shy,
You fell off the track and I know why,
But get back on and aim for the sky,
Don't let anyone make you feel you can't try,
The sky is limitless so reach up high,
So spread your wings and start to fly,
Before the rest of your life passes you by,
You're such a good kid you try not to lie,
Sometimes it's hard, but I know you'll get by,
You're the brightest star in the dark sky.

How Do I Know If I'm Being Abused

There are four types of abuse and they are as follows:

- Neglect
- Emotional abuse
- Physical abuse
- Sexual abuse

Each form of abuse is just as serious as the other. Although the signs of a child being abused are not always easy to see, they all leave scares. Some scars are visible, mental scars are also left behind and can be harder to deal or live with and can affect the child throughout the rest of his or her life. Below are the different forms of abuse in detail, and if you fall into one of these categories, I urge you please get some help. Don't do it because I am telling you to, but do it because you deserve a good fear-free life.
The abuses listed are in no particular order.

Neglect: If you are being neglected, you might not realise this is a form of abuse, but I can promise you, neglect is abuse. If your parents are letting you go hungry and are not there to wash your clothes or clean the house, or if they are out of the house and you are home alone and/or your parents are in the house but are busy and you have no supervision from an appropriate adult, this is neglect. And just because the signs are not always easy to see, it does not mean this is not happening.

Emotional Abuse: Just like neglect, if you are being emotionally abused, you might not know it. This form of abuse includes being

- ignored for long periods of time as a punishment,
- regularly yelled at for no reason or pulled down,
- called names and made to feel worthless,
- denied love such as being told 'I love you' and starved from any loving emotional connection, and
- being allowed to watch violence or another form of abuse to others such as your siblings.

I remember when I was a child I often had to watch my dad hurt my mom's cats because he didn't like them and he liked to watch me break my heart.

These are all examples of emotional abuse.

Physical Abuse: You might have a better idea of what this consists of—being hit, kicked, punched, and even head butted and hair pulled. Being hit does not have to be with hands or fists. It could be with things like a belt or a shoe or anything if it's used as a weapon. When I lived with my dad, I used to get held upside down by the ankle and my head pushed into the toilet and the chain flushed, or I would be told to drink out of a 2-litre bottle and whatever happened I would not be allowed to stop drinking. Then my dad would squeeze the bottle I would drink until I went light-headed and collapsed on the ground, coughing and gasping for air, so being drowned is also abuse along with strangulation and suffocation. Although being stabbed or body parts being cut off or having cigarettes being stubbed out on your skin is a little rarer, it sadly is only too real for some unfortunate children.

Sexual Abuse: There are certain things about sexual abuse that you may already know, things like intercourse. Body contact is when you yourself are being touched in the most intimate places of your body. If you are being forced to touch someone else's intimate places, this is also sexual abuse. There are other ways you could have been sexually abused, ways you might not know about. They are less obvious to some people. If you are being exposed to some sexual material like magazines or watching other people having sex, even if you yourself are not being touched, it does not matter—*it is sexual abuse*.

Now I have pointed out just some of the forms of abuse, so now I hope you have a better understanding of abuse, and if you are being abused, then you truly need to find an adult you can trust and with whom you are as comfortable as you could possibly be under the circumstances and tell that person everything. If you don't know anyone you can talk to, you need to go to the nearest police station and talk to them. But please, for your own sake, find the strength I know you have inside yourself and stand up and put a stop to abuse.

Everything I have said in these pages I believe to be the truth through my own experiences.

What Happens Next

For me, once I told the teacher, I went straight back to my lessons, and it wasn't until about an hour later that the teacher came, took me out of my class, and took me to her office where my social worker was waiting for me. I told the social worker everything that I had told the teacher. It wasn't easy to talk. I felt sick in the stomach. I was shaking and crying uncontrollably. But I knew it was now or never. After I finished saying what I needed to say, something dawned on me—I couldn't breathe, my mouth went dry, and I thought I was going to wee myself. All I managed to say was, 'I can't go home. He'll kill me.' It was then I reassured that I wasn't going home. I was going to go somewhere safe.

After school, I spent some time at the social worker's office and then I was taken to the foster placement he had arranged for me. Over the next week, I had to make written statements, and I was taken to the police station and photos were taken of all my bruises. It was embarrassing, but I kept telling myself that I will never see these people again and that helped a little.

The police and the social workers were very kind and did all they could to make me feel less frightened. And everything that was going to happen was explained to me throughout the whole case. From the beginning to the end, I believe they were honest with me and that also helped so much. I know you're scared of the unknown, but it is all worth it in the end. My only regret was I did not do it sooner. I could have stopped everything happening if only I had spoken up sooner. I don't want you to have any regrets like me, so that's why I am encouraging you to go and get help now today.

This is how things happened for me, so when you speak out about your situation, things might happen differently. It all depends on your personal circumstances. For example, I already had a social worker, so I knew who I was talking to. I told a teacher at school. You might tell someone else, so things might be a little different, but it doesn't matter because the outcome is the most important thing to focus on.

Useful Contacts

Childline
Phone 24/7 0800 1111
http://www.childline.org.uk/
Young people can phone trained counsellors to get advice on abuse.

Papyrus
Phone 0800 068 4141
http://www.papyrus-uk.org/
Teenagers and young dealing with depression, emotional distress, and suicide

Get connected
Helpline 0808 808 4994
http://www.getconnected.org/
Free confidential advice for young people on any subject.

NSPCC
helpline 0808 800 5000
http://www.nspcc.org.uk/

If you are in any immediate danger, you can phone 999. If you are at home, you can phone 999 from your house phone. And if you are not in a position where you can talk, you can leave the receiver off the base and the operator will record everything that she can hear, and the police will be dispatched out to your home straightaway.

You can either phone or speak to any of these numbers in confidentiality, but if the person believes you are in danger, they will have to tell the police or the social services, and a full investigation will be carried out. If they are going to break the confidentiality, then they would tell you so first.

Ways to Talk

I fully understand that speaking those words 'I Am being abused' can be the hardest thing you may have to do in your life. So I want to show you some other ways to speak.

Write it down
Try to write the things you are experiencing. You don't have to write a novel—just highlight what is happening in your life and pass the note on to a doctor, teacher, school nurse, even a police officer walking the street. But don't forget to add your name, address, and who the abuser is—because the last thing you want is for the police to knock onto your door and talk to your mom if it's your mom who is abusing you. So don't call your abuser Mr Z or Mrs Q.

Phone a helpline
If you feel like you can't talk to someone face to face, then maybe talking over the phone is the way to go. There are specially trained counsellors on the helplines, and they offer you safe, friendly advice.

Internet
You can also speak to people on the Net. It is the same as using the helplines—only you're typing and that can also be a way to go. I know some people are more comfortable when they don't have to talk at all, but you understand that you will have to speak to someone face to face at one point.

Questions You May Have

1) Do I have to go into foster care?
   Not all children go into foster care. It depends on your personal circumstances that surround your case. Many children are able to stay at home with their parents and work can be done with the parents to help them understand where they are going wrong and how to be the best that they can be.

2) What happens if I'm allowed to go home but I don't want to?
   Nobody will make you do something you don't want to or are not comfortable with. It's all about you and making you feel safe and secure.

3) What happens if I'm not happy in my placement?
   All you need to do if you're not happy is talk to your social worker. Explain why you're not happy, and they will do everything to resolve the issues you are facing. If your issues cannot be resolved, you may have to be placed in another placement.

4) Do I get to see my parents?
   This depends again on your individual circumstances. It can happen where the child wants to see their parents, but the parents do not want to see the child anymore. Also it happens where the parents want to see the child but the child refuses to see the parents. So if you are granted contact and the parents agree, then it's up to you to accept it. You do not have to go.

5) How is the contact set up?

If the contact is face to face, then it can be one of two ways. The first is supervised, and this is where you are with the social worker or with one of their assistants whilst you see your parents, or it can be unsupervised which is where you are alone with your parents at a place agreed beforehand.

If you are granted unsupervised but you're not comfortable with this decision, you should let your social worker know, and things can be rearranged to suit you.

6) What happens if I don't want to see my parents?

If you don't want to see your parents, then you don't have to. You should not be made to feel like you have to go to a contact. You shouldn't feel like you need to please anybody. It's now time to think about yourself and what you want.

7) If the contact has to stop, do I get to say goodbye?

If for some reason the contact has to be stopped, your parents will be offered a final contact and so will you. But sometimes the parents don't show up not because they don't want the chance to say goodbye but because it can be just too hard, and if you do not want the final contact, it is your decision.

8) What other types of contact are there?

There are two other types of contact but which contact you get offered all depends on your individual circumstances.

Phone contact is when your parents are given the phone number of your foster carer's home and a time and day is pre-arranged, and they can phone you. This contact can sometimes happen alongside a face-to-face meeting. With the phone contact, your foster carer is allowed to listen in if they feel it necessary. This is to ensure you're not being intimidated.

Post box contact happens around once a year, and this is normally for parents who don't see their children, and they are allowed to send letters, cards, and photos but not money or presents. Then the child is allowed to reply back to the parents. The letters will be opened and read to check the content is not upsetting for the child.

9) Can I trust my foster carer?

You can talk to your carer about anything, but every foster carer is required to keep a diary, and they have to fill it in every day with things you say and do. These rules are set by the social workers to monitor your health and to monitor any concerns they might have about you. The diary is then showed to the social worker on a regular basis, and when meetings come up, then the report is written from the information in the diary.

Lightning Source UK Ltd.
Milton Keynes UK
UKOW05n0127151113

221099UK00002B/32/P

9 781483 689807